Back
Old Time
Song Book
Words & Music To 40 Timeless Mountain Tunes. by Wayne Erbsen

Native Ground Music, Inc.
109 Bell Road
Asheville, NC 28805

Exclusive Distributors to the Music Trade:

Music Sales Corporation
225 Park Avenue South, New York, NY 10003 USA

Music Sales Limited
8/9 Frith Street, London W1V 5TZ England

Music Sales Pty. Limited
27 Clarendon Street, Artarmon, Sydney NSW 2064 Australia

The publisher has conducted an exhaustive search to locate the publisher or copyright owners of the tunes in this book. However, in the event we have inadvertently published a copyrighted composition without proper acknowledgment, we advise the copyright owner to contact us so that we may give appropriate credit in future editions.

Order No. WE 10000   ISBN 0-9629327-0-1

CONTENTS

SINGING AND PLAYING
THE OLD-TIME SONGS

Contrary to popular belief, you don't have to have a good voice to sing the old-time songs. (Read that over to yourself several times and make sure you've got it.) Many people are scared stiff to sing. Some would rather run naked through the city park in broad daylight than to stand there and sing a song. A funny world we live in.

The fact is, anybody with or without a set of tonsils who can mumble, whisper, or talk, can sing. You don't have to go to the conservatory to sing the old-fashioned songs. Just roll up your sleeves, take a firm grip of this book, and wrap your lungs around the first song that strikes your fancy.

Singing isn't something that all people take to immediately. Like anything else, it takes practice. Pack up your songbook and a lunch and head out to the nearest mountaintop, rice paddy, or pasture. Cows love music and make a wonderful audience. Test out your singing on them. If they approve, try groundhogs, rabbits, and telephone poles. If you don't hear any complaints, you know you're singing on pitch. Good work!

The secret of singing is nothing short of projecting confidence in your voice. Even if you feel like shriveling up and hiding behind the barn when you open your mouth to sing, belt it out anyway. Volume will make up for any lack of tone and pitch.

Keep in mind that most of the musicians who pioneered old-time music on radio and on records had untrained voices. Their natural way of singing must have sounded pretty funny to the recording engineers who practically had to hold their fingers in their ears while they listened to some of the would-be singers squawk into the microphone. The country people who bought their records as fast as the clerk could lay them on the counter didn't care. They wanted music that sounded like *them*. They wanted the down home, home-made tunes and songs; nothing fancy. So old-time music has a down-to-earthness about it that lets anybody join in. You don't need a musical pedigree to sing the old songs.

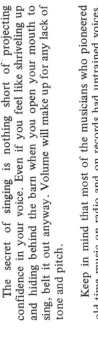

Photo by Blanton Owen

ODELL COCKERHAM, TOMMY JARRELL, EVA COCKERHAM, and FRED COCKERHAM

SINGING IN THE RIGHT KEY

The first old-time music was the old ballads, which were sung without accompaniment. Singers would pitch a song so they could sing both the highest and lowest notes with ease. When singers later tried to sing along with the fiddler, they often found that they practically had to stand on a chair to reach notes that were often out of their range. This is why some of the singing on the old records sounded almost like the shriek of air being slowly released from a balloon.

Here is a guide to help you approximate the key to sing the songs.

> Average male voice: Key of G A C D E
>   is **EQUAL** to
>
> Average female (or
> high male voice):   Key of C D F G A

In other words, if an average male voice sings a song in G, for example, an average female or high male singer would most likely sing it in C, and so on. This is only a rough guide, but will help you get close to where you want to sing a song.

Before you start to sing a song, hum or sing a little of the tune to try to find the highs and lows of the melody. This will help you to determine the proper key for singing. (People will laugh at you while you are doing this.) Then bribe the fiddler with a jug of moonshine liquor to play in your key. Be firm with him

Once you know the keys of your favorite songs, memorize them for future reference, or jot them down in your book. Knowing the key of a song will save precious time and the embarrassment of trying to sing a song out of your range.

The songs in this book are written out in keys that should be comfortable to the average male singer. If songs seem too low or too high, you will need to find other keys to sing in.

TRANSPOSING YOUR CHORDS

Should you decide to sing in a different key than is written in the book, you will need to change or "transpose" your chords. Most songs only have three chords. Changing keys merely means finding the new chords for the key you want to be in. Here is a handy chart to help you transpose.

Key of	I	IV	V
G	G	C	D
A	A	D	E
C	C	F	G
D	D	G	A
E	E	A	B

To use this chart, just select the key you want to be in, and your new chords are listed on the right. To understand what we mean by "I", "IV", and "V", turn to *Oh Them Golden Slippers* on page 8. The G is the "I" (one) chord, the D is the "V" (five) chord, and the C is the "IV" (four) chord. After you get used to these symbols, transposing will be a snap. In case you have forgotten your guitar chords, we have listed them for you on the inside back cover.

SINGING WITH AN INSTRUMENT

When you start singing you don't want to stand up there all by yourself. This book is too small to hide behind so the next best thing is to hold a guitar in front of you. Strumming a guitar will take some of the attention away from your singing, which may be good for now. Picking a banjo or mandolin will also work, but a guitar is the best instrument to play while singing.

USING A CAPO

A capo is an elastic or metal device which clamps on the neck of the guitar or banjo and raises the pitch of the instrument. It is an essential tool for the singer and helps you to play in keys that are most comfortable to sing in. Buy one.

To use it, merely clamp or tie it around the neck of your instrument at the second fret if a song seems too low or too high to sing. If the song is still out of your range, slide it up a fret or two until the song sings easily for your voice. Don't try to sing all your songs in the same key. If you find you need to slide your capo higher than the fifth fret, your guitar will sound like a cigar box strung with rubber bands. In that case check with the chord chart above, and select the next key down on the list. Try again.

OLD-TIME SONGS

The style that we refer to as "old-time music" is actually composed of many diverse elements. In the *Backpocket Old-Time Songbook*, we have organized these elements into eight major categories of old-time songs. As you sing your way through the book, these categories will unfold before you.

Courtesy of John Edwards Memorial Foundation

UNCLE DAVE MACON

MINSTREL SONGS

Old-time music draws much of its inspiration from the songs of the minstrels. Starting in about 1842, a minstrel craze swept America. Black-faced minstrels strumming banjos, sawing on fiddles, shaking rattles and beating on drums staged shows across America's east coast. Performing everywhere from the concert stage to Mississippi riverboats, these minstrels had a profound effect on American music.

Some of the early minstrels such as E.P. Christy and Joel Sweeney actually visited southern plantations to learn songs and banjo techniques from black slaves. Others may have picked up plantation music from freed slaves living in the North. The demand for new minstrel songs was so great that songwriters like Dan Emmett and Stephen Foster started cranking out new minstrel songs that even then sounded old. Most of the minstrel songs are long forgotten. A few, however, have been preserved not only as cherished memories of the past, but because they are just plain old good songs. Some of the earliest recordings of old-time music reflect this affection for the songs of the minstrels.

DANCE TUNES

Without serious contention, the fiddle is the backbone of old-time music. Brought over from Europe with the earliest settlers, it was portable and could be tucked under the arm or stowed under a wagon seat for a westward journey. Though some God-fearing people thought the fiddle was the instrument of the devil and referred to it as "the devil's box," many others held the fiddle in high esteem. Not only could he accompany some of the old ballads, but, most important, he could provide the music for dances. In the years before the guitar and banjo became popular, the fiddle was often the only instrument that could play for dancing. The only help he might get would be from the mouth of a Mason jar containing homemade spirits.

The tunes the first fiddlers played were, like the fiddle itself, brought over from Europe. It wasn't long before fiddlers composed new tunes or recombined the old ones. Gradually, words were added to some of the tunes and an occasional fiddler would holler out a verse or two to break up the monotony of playing for the long dances. Many of these verses were made up on the spot and just as quickly forgotten. Others, called "floating verses," drifted carelessly from tune to tune. Yelling out verses to fiddle tunes over the heads of a dancing mob did not tend to encourage beautiful tone nor delicate phrasing, but it was a start, nonetheless.

BALLADS

The singing of old ballads was the first old-time music in America. Brought over from England with the early immigrants, these ballads were treasured keepsakes from home. Sung unaccompanied, they told stories that often went on for twenty verses or more.

It was the women, far more than the men, who sang the old ballads. The menfolk, apparently, were much more interested in trying to get a squawk or two out of a fiddle. When it came time to pass their music on to their children, the women generally taught their daughters the ballads and the men handed down their fiddles to their sons.

Photo by David Holt

DELLIE NORTON

Photo by Wayne Erbsen

KNOCKDOWN TUNES

A "knockdown tune" is a rough and tumble banjo song that is likely to be played at breakneck tempos. Banjoists who played these old pieces generally played in a style variously known as clawhammer, thumb-cocking, rapping, frailing, and banging the banjo. It is also known as the "knockdown style." As these names imply, the banjoist would strike the strings with a rather ferocious stroke that would cause the strings to nearly jump off the banjo. This rhythmic style was created to back up the fiddler at dances long before mail order houses made guitars available. But knockdown banjo playing was far more versatile than merely providing rhythm for dances. It could easily be used to accompany all manner of songs by laying down a firm rhythmic foundation while at the same time playing melodies to compliment the singing of the old songs.

TICKLIN' SONGS

Ticklin' songs are nothing more or less than songs that make you laugh. Country people have always enjoyed a good laugh, even if the joke's on them.

OLD-FASHIONED PARLOR SONGS

The 1890's was the heyday of the sentimental ballad. These old-fashioned songs were not played so much in the taverns and road houses but in the parlor on the family piano. In the evening the whole family would gather around the piano and they would sing along as mother played the popular sheet music pieces of the day. Many of these sentimental songs were taken up by country singers who weren't ashamed to shed a tear over a sad song. These songs remained popular in the rural South long after they had gone out of style in the urban North.

LONESOME TUNES

Life in the mountains was often a lonely existence. Although there were dance tunes to perk things up, many of the slower songs had a mighty lonesome sound. To get this sound, the banjos were often tuned in "sawmill tuning" (gDGCD) and the fiddles in "cross tuning" (AEAE). The singers would shade their voices toward the minor sounding songs. The results might be called "mountain blues."

GOSPEL SONGS

Gospel songs have been an essential part of old-time music from the very beginning. Virtually all of the early singers learned the rudiments of music in church or from singing-school teachers who often traveled the country by horseback. These teachers would stop in a community and teach note reading as well as "shaped-note" singing. Many times such classes constituted the only formal instruction that most people ever had. The gospel songs are especially singable because they don't depend on instruments to make them sound good. With so many great gospel songs to choose from, only the best songs survive.

OH, THEM GOLDEN SLIPPERS

Even though minstrel shows of the nineteenth century tried to portray life and music on the plantation, there were few actual blacks performing in minstrel troups. One exception was a company of black minstrels who called themselves the Original Georgia Minstrels. One of the members was the educated and talented James A. Bland. Bland had numerous compositions to his credit, including *Oh, Them Golden Slippers, Carry Me Back to Old Virginny*, and *Hand Me Down My Walking Cane*. With its publication in 1879, *Golden Slippers* immediately became popular and was soon taken up by other minstrel shows. When old-time fiddlers got a hold of the song, they turned it into a popular tune to play for dances. While most fiddle tunes are played in only one key, *Golden Slippers* is commonly played either in G, D, or A. Fiddlers often play it as a twin fiddle showpiece.

Courtesy of Memorial Library, Mars Hill College

Photo by William Barnhill

Courtesy of Special Collections, Hunter Library, Western Carolina University

QUILL ROSE

JAMES A. BLAND

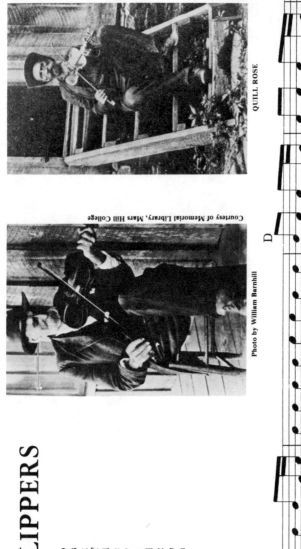

Sprightly

1. Oh, my gold-en slip-pers are laid a-way, 'Cause I don't ex-pect to wear 'em till my wed-ding day, And my long-tailed coat that I love so well I will
   And my long white robe that I bought last June, I'm goin' to get it changed 'cause it fits too soon, And the old grey horse that I used to ride I will

2. Oh, my old banjo hangs on the wall,
'Cause it ain't been tuned since way last fall,
But the old folks say we will have a good time,
When we ride up in the chariot in the morning.
There's old Brother Ben and Sister Luce,
They will telegraph the news to Uncle 'Bacco Juice,
What a great camp meeting there will be that day,
When we ride up in the chariot in the morning.
Chorus:

3. Goodby children, I will have to go,
Where the rain don't fall or the wind don't blow.
And your ulster coats, why you will not need
When you ride up in the chariot in the morning.
But the golden slippers must be neat and clean
And your age must be just sweet sixteen,
And your white kid gloves you will have to wear,
When you ride up in the chariot in the morning.
Chorus:

DIXIE

DAN EMMETT

Briskly

1. I wish I was in the land of cot - ton, Old times there are not for - got - ten, Look a - way, look a - way, look a - way, Dix - ie Land. In Dix - ie - land where I was born in, Ear - ly on one frost - y morn - in', Look a - way, look a - way, look a - way, Dix - ie Land.

Chorus:

I wish I was in Dix - ie, Hoo - ray! Hoo - ray! In Dix - ie Land I'll take my stand, To live and die in Dix - ie. A - way, a - way, a - way down south in Dix - ie; A - way, a - way, a - way down south in Dix - ie.

People don't whistle *Dixie* like they used to. Written by Dan Emmett for the New York minstrel stage in 1859, it became the equivalent of the "Southern National Anthem." It was played for Jefferson Davis' inauguration, and as rebel soldiers marched into battle, they sang *Dixie.*

Even though *Dixie* was the battle hymn of the Confederacy, it was extremely popular in the North, as well. It was, in fact, one of Abraham Lincoln's favorite songs. In later years *Dixie* was associated with the image of the old South, and it became unfashionable to sing it. Perhaps when the scars of the struggle for equality have fully healed, *Dixie* will again be as popular as in the days when Dan Emmett so harmlessly composed it.

2. There's buckwheat cakes and Injun batter,
Makes you fat or a little fatter,
Look away, look away,
Look away, Dixie Land.

Then hoe it down and scratch your gravel,
To Dixie Land I'm bound to travel,
Look away, look away,
Look away, Dixie Land. *Chorus:*

ANGELINA BAKER

Angelina Baker comes to us from the pen of Stephen Foster. Published in 1850, it was not one of Foster's more popular songs. After seven years, in fact, Foster had earned only $16.87 for it. The song tells of the love of a slave for Angelina Baker, a beautiful young slave woman. Angelina is sold away and the slave consoles himself by beating on an old jawbone, an instrument that was used like a rattle.

Angelina Baker entered the repertoire of old-time music and has become a popular fiddle tune. As it was passed from hand to hand, the melody was changed and the title became *Angeline the Baker*. The words to the original song were forgotten and new words were made up to take their place. Here, again, are the original words to *Angelina Baker*.

STEPHEN C. FOSTER

Leisurely

1. Way down on the old plan-ta-tion that's where I was born; I used to beat the whole cre-a-tion hoe-ing in the corn. Oh, then I work and then I sing so hap-py all the day, Till An-ge-li-na Ba-ker came and stole my heart a-way.

Chorus: An-ge-li-na Ba-ker! An-ge-li-na Ba-ker's gone; She left me here to weep a tear, And beat on the old jaw-bone.

2. I've seen my Angelina in the springtime and the fall,
I've seen her in the cornfield, and I've seen her at the ball;
And every time I met her she was smiling like the sun,
But now I'm left to weep a tear cause Angelina's gone.
Chorus:

3. Angelina am so tall she never sees the ground,
She has to take a telescope to look down on the town.
Angelina likes the boys as far as she can see 'em,
She used to run old massa round to ax him for to free them.
Chorus:

4. Early in the morning of a lovely summer day,
I ax for Angelina and they say she's gone away.
I don't know where to find her cause I don't know
where she's gone,
She left me here to weep a tear and beat on the old jawbone.
Chorus:

I'M GWINE BACK TO DIXIE

I'm Gwine Back to Dixie paints a touching picture of an ex-slave who longs for home. Written in 1874 by C.A. White, the song has been performed widely on the minstrel stage as well as on early early country music records. Uncle Dave Macon recorded it for Vocalion on May 9, 1927 and it is his version we present here. This song would sound good with a little harmony singing on the chorus.

Photo by Wayne Erbsen

C. A. WHITE

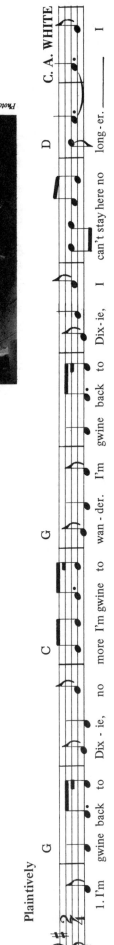

Plaintively

1. I'm gwine back to Dix-ie, no more I'm gwine to wan-der. I'm gwine back to Dix-ie, I can't stay here no long-er.

miss the old plan-ta-tion, my home, and my re-la-tions. My heart's turned back to Dix-ie, and I must go.

2. I've hoed in fields of cotton, I've worked upon the river.
   I used to think if I'd get off, I'd never go back, no, never.
   But time has changed the old man; his head is bending low,
   His heart's turned back to Dixie and I must go.   *Chorus:*

3. I miss my hog and hominy, my pumpkin and red gravy.
   My appetite is fading, so says old Uncle Davy.
   If my friends forsake me I pray the Lord to take me.
   My heart's turned back to Dixie and I must go.   *Chorus:*

KINGDOM COMING
(Year of the Jubilo)

Early in the Civil War a young man named Henry Clay Work showed up at music publishers Root & Cady with the manuscript of *Kingdom Coming* in his hand. Poorly clad, he did not look like the great composer that he was. George Root, the publisher, did not expect much as he casually looked over the manuscript. He soon realized that here was a great piece of musical satire that perfectly fit the times. In April of 1862 the song was performed by Christy's Minstrels and went on to become one of the most popular songs of the nineteenth century. Even after Lee's surrender at Appomattox, Union soldiers sang *The Year of Jubilio*, as it came to be called, as they marched into Richmond. I have recently heard a "Muzak" version of the song wafting through the air in a public building.

HENRY C. WORK

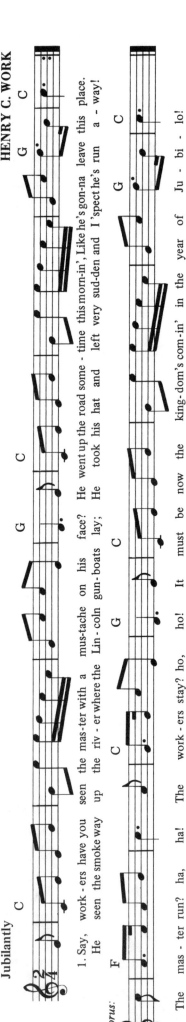

Jubilantly

1. Say, work-ers have you seen the mas-ter with a mus-tache on his face? He went up the road some-time this morn-in', Like he's gon-na leave this place.
He seen the smoke way up the riv-er where the Lin-coln gun-boats lay; He took his hat and left very sud-den and I 'spect he's run a-way!

Chorus:

The mas-ter run? ha, ha! The work-ers stay? ho, ho! It must be now the king-dom's com-in' in the year of Ju-bi-lo!

2. He's six-foot one way, two-foot the other and he weighs three hundred pounds.
His coat so big he couldn't pay the tailor and it wouldn't go halfway around.
He drill so much they call him Captain and he got so dreadful tanned,
I 'spect he'll try and fool them Yankees for to think he's contraband. *Chorus:*

3. The overseer, he make us trouble and he drive us 'round a spell,
We lock him up in the smokehouse celler, with the key throwed down the well.
The whip is lost and handcuff broken but the master'll have his pay,
He's old enough, big enough, ought to know better than to want to run away. *Chorus:*

JORDAN IS A HARD ROAD TO TRAVEL

Jordan Is a Hard Road to Travel is one of the goofiest songs in the old-time music repertoire. Written originally as a minstrel tune by Dan Emmett while living in Cincinnati, Ohio in 1853, it was adopted by old-time musicians who freely made up new verses while generally retaining the original chorus. The results were recorded in October of 1928 by Riley Puckett, who renamed it *On The Other Side of Jordan.* **DAN EMMETT**

Exuberantly

1. If you want to do well go down the ho-tel, Get your room and your board on cred-it.___ When they ask you for your pay just tell them right a-way To get it on the oth-er side of Jor-dan.___

Chorus:

Haul off your o-ver-coat and roll up your sleeves, Haul off your o-ver-coat and roll up your sleeves, Jor-dan is a hard road to trav-el.___ Jor-dan is a hard road to trav-el, Jor-dan is a hard road to trav-el, I be-lieve. And they found it on the other side of Jordan.

2. Daddy caught a turkey in the woods the other day
And he put him in the pot for to cook him
He jerked back his head and he knocked off the lid
And he gobbled on the other side of Jordan. *Chorus:*

3. David and Goliath had a fight the other day
They found one thing for certain
He hit Goliath on the head with a bar of salt soap
And they found it on the other side of Jordan. *Chorus:*

LITTLE LOG CABIN IN THE LANE

By the 1890's it was relatively easy to walk into a store and buy a handful of classical and light opera cylinders or discs then being produced. Rural southerners, however, found that record producers in New York had not seen fit to record southern string band music, which was then the rage across the South. This changed, however, in 1923, when Polk Brockman, the Atlanta distributor for Okeh records, realized the commercial potential of producing hillbilly records. He got John Carson, a popular Georgia fiddler, moonshiner, and local character, to record for Okeh. Carson recorded *Little Log Cabin in the Lane* along

with *The Old Hen Cackled and the Rooster's Going to Crow*. To the surprise of Okeh record producer **Ralph Peer**, the songs were a success, and marked the beginning of what was soon to be an entire record industry devoted to old-time country music.

The song itself was written in 1871 by William Shakespeare Hays, who died long before he knew that his song had made country music history.

Courtesy of North Carolina Division of Archives and History

WILLIAM SHAKESPEARE HAYS

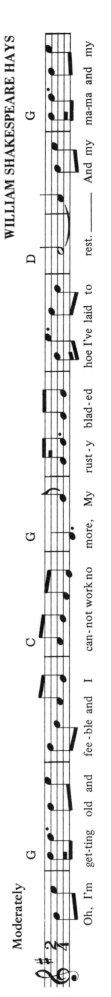

Moderately

Oh, I'm get-ting old and fee-ble and I can-not work no more, My rust-y blad-ed hoe I've laid to rest._____ And my ma-ma and my pa-pa they are sleep-ing side by side While their spir-its now are roam-ing with the blessed.— Oh, the chim-ney's fall-ing down, and the roof is tum-bled in,

let-ting in the sun-shine and the rain.— And the on-ly friend I've got now is this lit-tle old dog of mine In that lit-tle old log cab-in in the lane.—

2. Oh the happiest times to me was not many years ago,
My friends all used to gather 'round the door.
They would sing and dance at night while I played that old banjo
But alas, I cannot play it any more.   *Chorus:*

3. Well, the paths they have growed up that led us 'round the hill;
The fences have all gone to decay.
The creeks they have dried up where we used to go to mill;
Things have changed their course another way.   *Chorus:*

4. Well I ain't got long to stay here, what little time I've got
I'll try to rest content while I remain.
Until death shall call his dog and me to find a better home
Than the little old log cabin in the lane.   *Chorus:*

WATERMELON ON THE VINE

Here is a minstrel-flavored song originally entitled *Watermelon Smiling on the Vine* written by T.P. Westendorf in 1882. The song was a favorite of many old-time string bands and was recorded by the likes of Uncle Dave Macon and the Monroe Brothers. The version presented here comes to us from a rendition by the Skillet Lickers, who recorded it in the 1920's.

T. P. WESTENDORF

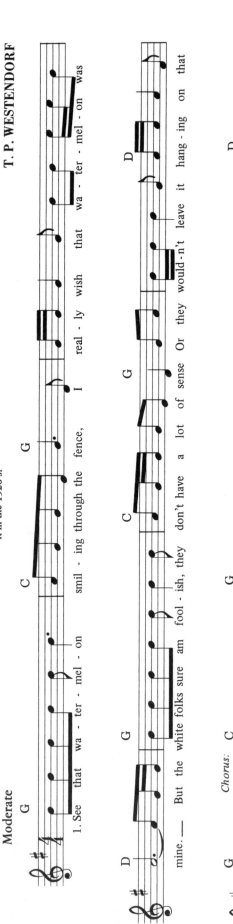

Moderate

1. See that wa-ter-mel-on smil-ing through the fence, I real-ly wish that wa-ter-mel-on was mine.— But the white folks sure am fool-ish, they don't have a lot of sense Or they would-n't leave it hang-ing on that vine.

Chorus: Now ham-bone am sweet chick-en am good Pok chop is so ver-y, ver-y, fine, Put

give me, oh give me, Oh, how I wish you would, That wa‑ter‑mel‑on hang‑ing on the vine.

2. You talk about your apples, your peaches, and your pears,
   'Simmons growing on the tree;
   But bless your heart, my honey, you am the gal for me,
   Or they wouldn't leave it hanging on that vine.

   Chorus :

3. I went to get that melon, it was on one Sunday night,
   Stars they had just begin to shine.
   But when I left that old man's field I left there in a run
   But I never left that melon on that vine.

   Chorus:

GID TANNER AND HIS SKILLET‑LICKERS with RILEY PUCKET AND CLAYTON McMICHEN

CUMBERLAND GAP

In the old days, no self-respecting fiddler would leave a dance without first playing a rendition of *Cumberland Gap*. The gap itself is a gorge in the Cumberland Mountains where Kentucky, Tennessee, and Virginia meet. Discovered in 1748, it was named after the Duke of Cumberland. Daniel Boone blazed the Wilderness Road through the gap in 1769 and fought pitched battles with Indians there. During the Civil War the gap was strategically important and both sides took turns capturing it.

The tune *Cumberland Gap* is nearly always played in G, but verses vary widely, depending on who you hear sing it. This version is from the singing of Tommy Jarrell.

Full throttle

Traditional

1. Lay down, boys, and take a little nap; We're all going down to Cumberland Gap.

2. I'm going back to Cumberland Gap
   To see my granny and my grandpap.

3. Save my money and I'll buy me a farm;
   I'll raise sweet potatoes as long as your arm.

4. Old Aunt Cate, Old Aunt Sal,
   Old Miss York's got a pretty little gal.

5. Old man Cate if he don't care
   Leave my demijohn sittin' right there.

6. If he ain't here when I get back
   I'll raise hell in Cumberland Gap.

7. I'll lay down and take a little nap;
   Wake up sober in Cumberland Gap.

Photo by David Holt

TOMMY JARRELL

COTTON-EYED JOE

Virtually every old-time fiddler knows some version of *Cotton-eyed Joe*. The verses portray Cotton-eyed Joe as a wily old feller who plays the fiddle and gets into his own peculiar brand of mischief. Apparently, he was plagued with cataracts, hence the nickname "Cotton-eyed Joe."

This version comes from the great fiddler from Mt. Airy, North Carolina, Tommy Jarrell. Jarrell gathered together this set of words from musicians near his home, and particularly credits Ray Braidy with teaching him some of them. Some fiddlers play the tune in A, while others prefer it in the key of G. We have it written out for you in G to keep you from torturing your tonsils.

Traditional

Wide open

1. Way down yon-der a long time a-go, Dad-dy had a man called Cot-ton-eyed Joe. ——

Where did you come from; Where did you go? Where did you come from, Cot-ton-eyed Joe?

Chorus:

2. Made him a fiddle and made him a bow,
And they made a little tune called "Cotton-eyed Joe."

Chorus:

3. Cornstalk fiddle and a shoe string bow
And he played that tune called "Cotton-eyed Joe."

Chorus:

4. I fell down and stubbed my toe
Call for the doctor, Cotton-eyed Joe.

Chorus:

5. Would have been married long time ago
Hadn't a been for Cotton-eyed Joe.

Chorus:

BEACHARD SMITH

Photo by Maxine Kenny

BULLY OF THE TOWN

Bully of the Town has remained a favorite dance tune since it was first introduced in 1895. It is not a wide open "hoedown" dance tune like *Soldier's Joy*, but has a slower, more relaxed feeling to it. Many of the old timers used to play this tune in C, but we have it written out for you in the key of G.

Bully of the Town is unique among the old dance tunes in its chord progression. While many of the early southern mountain tunes more or less stayed on one chord, as in the case of *Cotton-eyed Joe*, *Bully of the Town* goes to chords like F sharp, which brings a frown to the face of most struggling guitar players. Some guitarists, like Riley Puckett, left out this difficult chord. If your fingers cry out in pain, you can leave it out too.

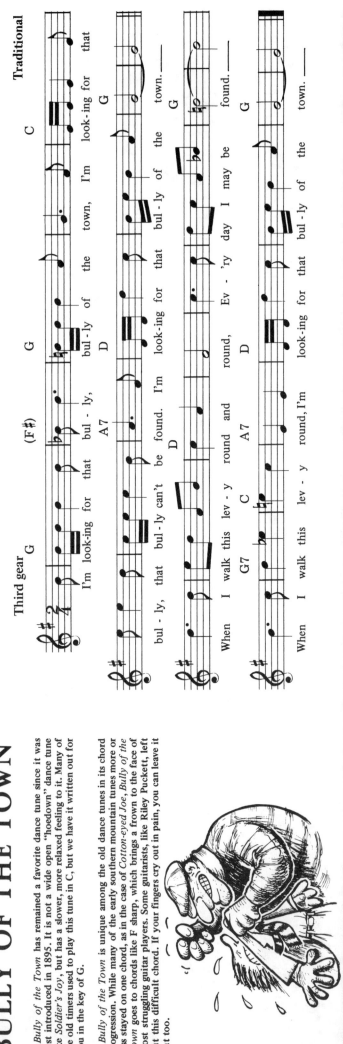

PRETTY SARO

Among the most beautiful of the old ballads is *Pretty Saro*. Probably originating in England many years before, it was collected on May 28, 1910 by Olive Dame Campbell from Mrs. Mackinney of Habersham County, Georgia. It is nearly always sung unaccompanied.

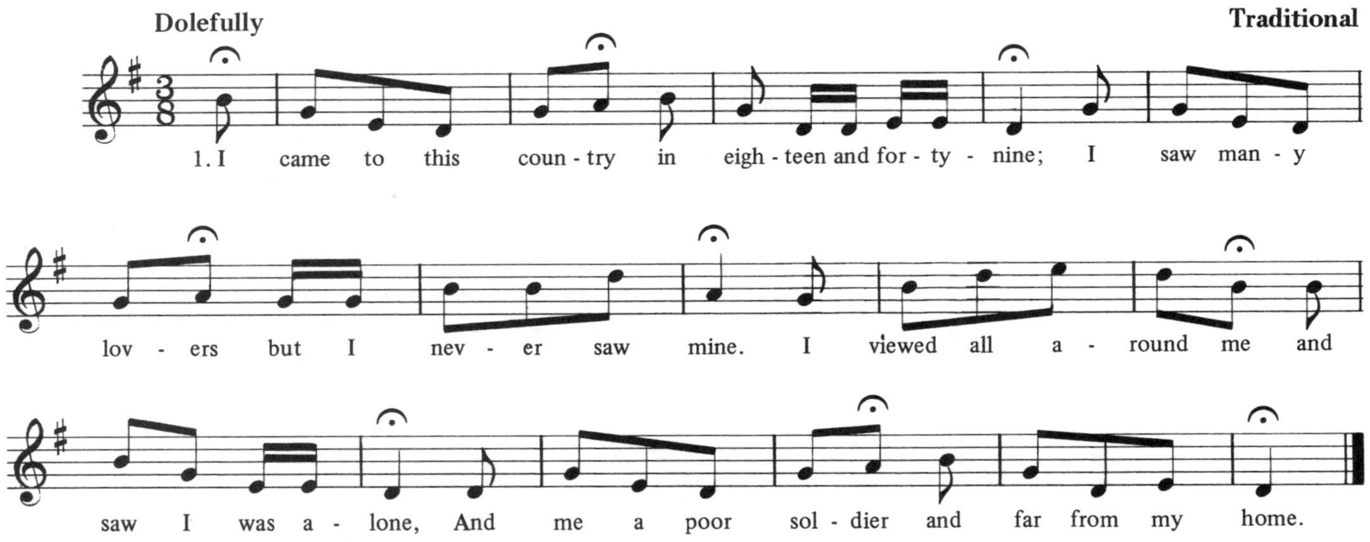

Dolefully
Traditional
1. I came to this coun - try in eigh - teen and for - ty - nine; I saw man - y
lov - ers but I nev - er saw mine. I viewed all a - round me and
saw I was a - lone, And me a poor sol - dier and far from my home.

2. It is not the long journey I'm dreading to go;
   Nor leaving the country for the debts that I owe.
   There's nothing that grieves me nor troubles my mind
   Like leaving pretty Saro, my darling, behind.

3. I wish I was a poet that could write a fine hand.
   I'd write my love a letter that she might understand.
   I'd send it by the waters, where the island overflows,
   And think on pretty Saro wherever I go.

4. Farewell, my dear father, likewise mother too,
   I am going to ramble this country all through.
   And when I get tired, I'll sit down and cry
   And think on pretty Saro with tears in my eyes.

WIND AND RAIN

Wind and Rain is one of the finest of the old ballads, albeit a little gory. It goes back several hundred years to England, and it is commonly sung under the title *Two Sisters*. Varients to this song abound and this one was taken from the singing of Dan Tate of Fancy Gap, Virginia.

Traditional

Dismally

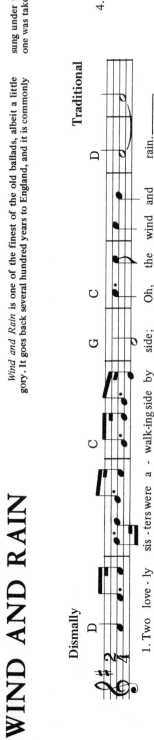

1. Two love-ly sis-ters were a - walk-ing side by side; Oh, the wind and rain. One pushed the oth - er in the wa - ters so—— deep And she cried a dread-ful wind and rain.——

2. She floated on down to the miller's mill pond;
   Oh, the wind and rain.
   She floated on down to the miller's mill pond,
   And she cried a dreadful wind and rain.

3. He hooked her up by the tail of her gown;
   Oh, the wind and rain.
   He hooked her up by the tail of her gown,
   And she cried a dreadful wind and rain.

4. He made fiddle strings of her long black hair;
   Oh, the wind and rain.
   He made fiddle strings of her long black hair;
   And she cried a dreadful wind and rain.

5. He made fiddle screws of her long fingerbones;
   Oh, the wind and rain.
   He made fiddle screws of her long finger bones,
   And she cried a dreadful wind and rain.

6. The only tune that the fiddle would play was;
   Oh, the wind and rain.
   The only tune that the fiddle would play,
   And she cried a dreadful wind and rain.

THE RAMBLING BOY

The Rambling Boy, also known as *The Rake and Rambling Boy,* is an old English ballad which was brought over to America with the early settlers and has remained popular through the years. This version was collected from Currence and Minnie Hammonds of Huttonsville, West Virginia.

Plaintively

Traditional

1. I was a rich, — but I — paid my — cit-y — Man-y a ram-bling boy; — I — did en - joy. — To Lon - don at the ball - room there. fare — And spent all my mon - ey cit - y — there.

2. It's there I married me a wife
   I loved her dearer than I did my life.
   I treated her both kind and gay
   And she caused me to rob on the road highway.

3. I robbed them all, I do declare,
   I robbed them all in deep despair.
   I robbed them of ten thousand pounds
   One night when I was a-rambling around.

4. I'll buy me a ticket for Greenville town;
   I'll get on the train and I'll sit down.
   Well, the wheels will roll and the whistle will blow.
   In five more days I'll be at home.

5. My mother said she weeps and mourns,
   My sister says she's left alone.
   My own true love in deep despair,
   With a pale red ribbon in her curly brown hair.

6. I have bright goods to carry me through;
   Three glittering swords and a pistol too.
   And a pretty fair girl for to pay my toll,
   With her diamond rings and her silver and gold.

7. When I'm dead and in my grave
   No more good liquor will I crave.
   On my tombstone I want it wrote
   Ten thousand gallons went down my throat.

ROCKINGHAM COUNTY ENTERTAINERS

DIAMOND JOE

Diamond Joe was first recorded by the Georgia Crackers in 1927. Although this song leaves us in suspense as to the identity of Diamond Joe, there is a different song, also entitled *Diamond Joe*, which paints a vivid picture of this rascal:

"His bread it was corn dodger
His meat I could not chaw
And he ran me near distracted
with the wagging of his jaw."

"And the telling of his stories
I'd like to let you know
There never was a rounder
Who lied like Diamond Joe."

If "our" Diamond Joe is any kin to this scalawag, I'm not sure I'd want him to "Come and get me."

Rollicking

Traditional

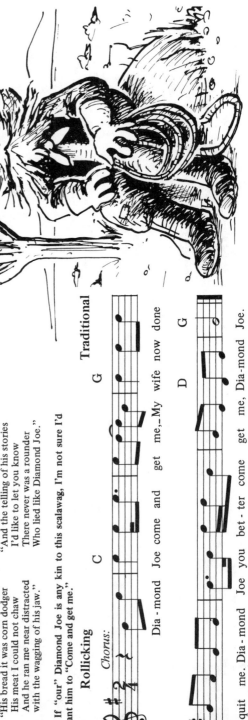

Dia - mond Joe come and get me,_My wife now done
quit me. Dia - mond Joe you bet - ter come get me, Dia - mond Joe.

1. I'm gonna buy me a sack of flour
   Cook a hoecake every hour.
   Diamond Joe, you better come get me, Diamond Joe.
   Chorus:

2. I'm gonna buy me a piece of meat,
   Cook me a slice once a week.
   Diamond Joe, you better come get me, Diamond Joe.
   Chorus:

3. I'm gonna buy me a sack of meal.
   Take a hoecake to the field.
   Diamond Joe, you better come get me, Diamond Joe.
   Chorus:

4. I'm gonna buy me a jug of whiskey,
   I'm gonna make my baby frisky.
   Diamond Joe, you better come get me, Diamond Joe.
   Chorus:

5. I'm gonna buy me a jug of rum,
   I'm gonna give my Ida some.
   Diamond Joe, better come get me, Diamond Joe.
   Chorus:

WILDWOOD FLOWER

If there is one song that deserves the title of "Hillbilly National Anthem," it is the *Wildwood Flower*. It is rare to play a show in the South without receiving at least one request to play the *Wildwood Flower*. It was the Carter Family's 1935 recording that made the song popular, but it was actually composed by Maud Irving and J.D. Webster and published in 1860 as *I'll Twine 'Mid the Ringlets*.

MAUD IRVING and
J.D. WEBSTER

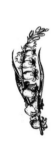

Painfully

1. I'll — twine 'mid the ring - lets of ra - ven black hair; The —
li - lies so pale and the ro - ses so fair. The — myr - tle so bright with an
em - er - ald hue, And the pale a - ron - a - tus with eyes of bright blue. —

2. I'll sing and I'll dance my laugh shall be gay,
   I'll cease this wild weeping, drive sorrow away;
   Tho' my heart is now breaking he never shall know,
   That his name made me tremble and my pale cheek to glow.

3. I'll think of him never, I'll be wildly gay,
   I'll charm every heart and the crowd I will sway.
   I'll live yet to see him regret the dark hour,
   When he won then neglected the frail wildwood flower.

4. He told me he loved me and promised to love
   Through ill and misfortune, all others above.
   Another has won him, Oh! misery to tell,
   He left me in silence no words of farewell!

5. He taught me to love him, he called me his flower,
   That blossom'd for him all the brighter each hour.
   But I woke from my dreaming, my idol was clay,
   My visions of love have all faded away.

DARLING NELLY GRAY

Darling Nelly Gray tells the tale of a young slave woman who is sold away in slavery while her lover pined away on the old Kentucky shore. It was written in 1856 by Benjamin Russell Hanby while still attending college. Hoping to get his song published, he innocently sent his song to a Boston publisher, Oliver Ditson & Co. Ditson turned the song into a nationwide hit and rewarded Hanby with a measly ten complimentary copies of the sheet music. Writing to complain, he was informed that he had earned the fame and Ditson the money, and that the score was even. Hanby never made a cent off this classic of old-time music.

BENJAMIN RUSSELL HANBY

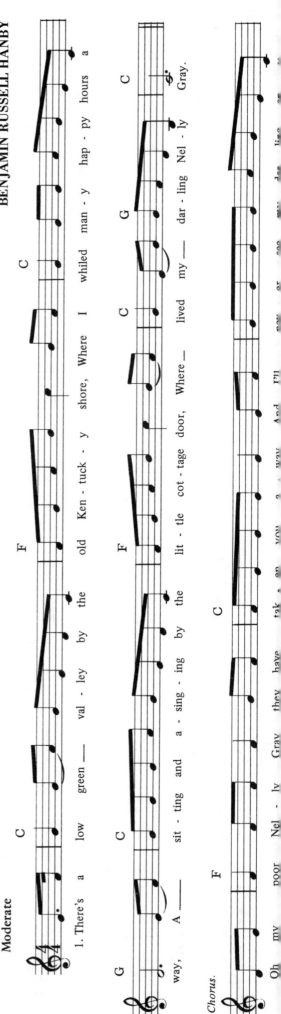

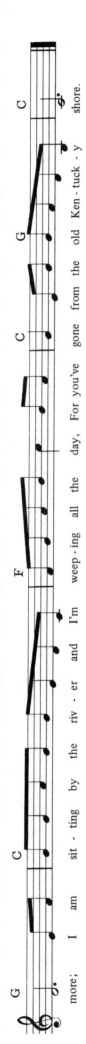

G C F C G C

I am sit-ting by the riv-er and I'm weep-ing all the day, For you've gone from the old Ken-tuck-y shore.

G

more;

2. One night I went to see her but she's gone, the neighbors say.
The white man bound her with his chain.
They have taken her to Georgia for to wear her life away,
As she toils in the cotton and the cane.
Chorus:

3. My canoe is under water and my banjo is unstrung
I'm tired of living any more
My eyes shall look downward and my songs shall be unsung
While I stay on the old Kentucky shore
Chorus:

4. My eyes are getting blinded and I cannot see my way.
Hark! There's somebody knocking at the door.
Oh! I hear the angels calling and I see my Nelly Gray.
Farewell to the old Kentucky shore.

Chorus to the last verse:
Oh my darling Nelly Gray, up in heaven there, they say.
That they'll never take you from me anymore.
I'm a coming, coming, coming, as the angels clear the way;
Farewell to the old Kentucky shore.

SOURWOOD MOUNTAIN

Traditional

An old timer living deep in the hills of southwest Virginia told me he knew the very mountain that is immortalized in *Sourwood Mountain*. He claimed that a young couple were about to be married so the young man climbed Sourwood Mountain and built them a cabin. On their wedding day he sang her this song that he had written.

Spirited

1. My true love lives up the hol - lar, Hey ho a - did - dle um day.
She won't come and I can't fol - ler, Hey ho a - did - dle um day.

Chorus:

Chick - ens crowin' on sour - wood moun - tain, Hey ho a - did - dle um day.
So many pretty girls, I can't count 'em, Hey ho a - did - dle um day.

2. My true love's a blue-eyed daisy, Hey ho a-diddle um day.
If I don't get her I'll go crazy, Hey ho a-diddle um day.

Chorus:

3. Big dogs bark and the little ones bite you, Hey ho a-diddle um day.
Big girls court and the little ones slight you, Hey ho a-diddle um day.

Chorus:

4. My true love lives up the river, Hey ho a-diddle um day.
A few more jumps and I'll be with her, Hey ho a-diddle um day.

Chorus:

BRAVEST COWBOY

As far as historians have been able to detect, cowboys have never been prevalent in the South, although cowboy hats are. Nonetheless, a footloose cowboy will occasionally appear in a song, throw his lariat, ride a bronc or two, and ride off into the sunset. *Bravest Cowboy* comes to us from Tommy Jarrell.

Ambling

Traditional

1. I am the brav-est cow-boy. That's ev-er tried the West. I've been all o-ver the Rock-ies. Got bul-lets in my breast.

2. In eighteen hundred and sixty-three,
I joined the immigrant band.
We marched from San Antonio
Down by the Rio Grand.

3. I went out on the prairie
And learned to rob and steal.
And when I robbed that cowboy;
How happy I did feel.

4. I wore a wide brim high hat,
My saddle too was fine.
And when I courted a pretty girl,
You bet I called her mine.

5. I courted her for beauty,
For love it was in vain,
'Til they carried me down to Dallas,
To wear a ball and chain.

GROUND HOG

The ground hog or woodchuck is a pesky little animal that is often found munching on your garden or seen lumbering along the highway. He is celebrated in this song which remains a standard in old-time music.

Catching a ground hog in the old days was an easy matter. One merely attached a wire to a long pole which was then twisted in the animal's coat while he lay huddled deep in his hole. Once caught by the wire, he could easily be pulled out and thrown in a sack where he soon became the guest of honor for supper.

Quay Smathers, an old timer from Canton, North Carolina, told how he used to catch ground hogs. He would sprinkle alum around a ground hog hole. The hole would soon pucker and squirt the surprised animal out of his hole. Before he could shake his tail, his hide was stretched over a banjo and he was playing *Cripple Creek*, or worse – *Ground Hog*.

33

Blithely

Traditional

Shoul-der up your gun and whis-tle up your dogs, Shoul-der up your gun and

whis-tle up your dogs, We're off to the woods for to catch a ground hog, Oh, ground____ hog.

2. Here comes granny walking on a cane,
   Here comes granny walking on a cane,
   Says she's gonna eat that ground hog's brain,
   Oh, ground hog.

3. Here comes Sal with a great long pole,
   Here comes Sal with a great long pole,
   Twist that whistle pig outta his hole,
   Oh, ground hog.

4. Here comes Sal with a snigger and a grin,
   Here comes Sal with a snigger and a grin,
   Ground hog grease all over her chin,
   Oh, ground hog.

5. I dug down but I didn't dig deep,
   I dug down but I didn't dig deep,
   There lay a whistle pig fast asleep,
   Oh, ground hog.

6. You eat up the meat and you save the hide,
   You eat up the meat and you save the hide,
   Makes the best shoe strings you ever tied,
   Oh, ground hog.

7. Put that hog in a big toe sack,
   Put that hog in a big toe sack,
   Bring him home swung down my back.
   Oh, ground hog.

8. Little piece of cornbread laying on the shelf,
   Little piece of cornbread laying on the shelf,
   If you want any more you can sing it yourself,
   Oh, ground hog.

OH MY LITTLE DARLING

Oh My Little Darling was collected by the Library of Congress from Thaddeus Willingham of Gulfport, Mississippi. As a boy, Willingham lived on a farm in Alabama where he learned to play the banjo and sing the old songs from ex-slaves who worked on the farm. This song makes a fine knock-down style banjo piece.

Traditional

Peppy

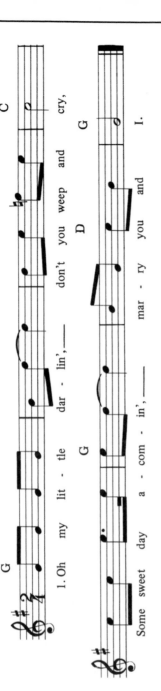

1. Oh my lit - tle dar - lin', don't you weep and cry,
Some sweet day a - com - in', mar - ry you and I.

2. Up and down the railroad, 'cross the county line,
   Pretty little girl's a-laughing, my wife is always cryin'.

3. Oh my little darlin' don't you weep and moan,
   Some sweet day a-comin', take my baby home.

4. Jimmy drives the wagon, Jimmy holds the line
   Kill yourself a-laughing, see them horses flying.

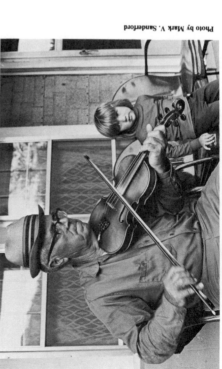

CORBETT STAMPER AND GRANDDAUGHTER

Photo by Mark V. Sandeford

THE YELLOW ROSE OF TEXAS

The Yellow Rose of Texas has been consistently popular since it was first published in 1858 by Firth Pond & Co. The author is identified only by the initials "J.K." and remains a mystery. Like *Dixie*, *The Yellow Rose of Texas* became a patriotic song during the Civil War and was sung by troops under General J.B. Hood, who commanded the Confederate's "Texas Brigade."

J. K.

Briskly

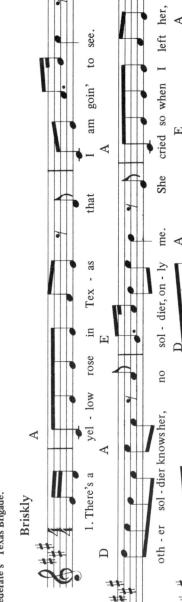

1. There's a yel - low rose in Tex - as that I am goin' to see. No oth - er sol - dier knows her, no sol - dier, on - ly me. She cried so when I left her, it like to broke my heart. And if I ev - er find her we nev - er more will part.

2. She's the sweetest rose of color this soldier ever knew.
Her eyes are bright as diamonds, they sparkle like the dew.
You may talk about your Dearest May and sing of Rosa Lee,
But the yellow rose of Texas beats the belles of Tennessee.

3. Where the Rio Grande is flowing and the starry skies are bright.
She walks along the river in the quiet summer night.
She thinks if I remember where we parted long ago,
I promised to come back again and not to leave her so.

4. Oh, now I'm going to find her for my heart is full of woe;
And we'll sing the song together that we sung so long ago.
We'll play the banjo gaily and we'll sing the songs of yore
And the yellow rose of Texas shall be mine forever more.

MILWAUKEE BLUES

Milwaukee Blues is Charlie Poole's composition about a hobo named Old Bill Jones. In putting the song together, Poole borrowed the last verse of *Casey Jones* and gave it a unique sprightly rhythm that makes you want to hop a freight and ride.

Traditional

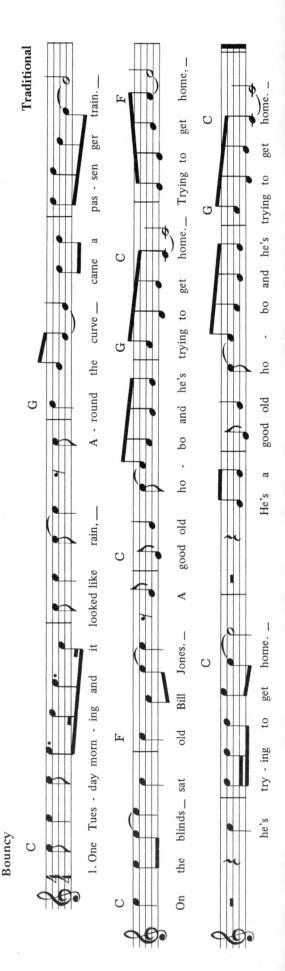

Bouncy

1. One Tues - day morn - ing and it looked like rain, — A - round the curve — came a pas - sen ger train. —

On the blinds — sat old Bill Jones. — A good old ho - bo and he's trying to get home. — Trying to get home, —

He's try - ing to get home. — He's a good old ho - bo and he's trying to get home. —

CHARLIE POOLE AND THE NORTH CAROLINA RAMBLERS

2. Way down in Georgia on a tramp
The roads are getting muddy and the leaves are getting damp.
I've got to catch a freight train to leave this town
'Cause they don't 'low no hoboes a-hanging around.

Hanging around, yes, hanging around,
They don't 'low no hoboes a-hanging around.

3. I left Atlanta one morning 'fore day
The brakeman said you'll have to pay.
I got no money but I'll pawn you my shoes;
I want to go west; I've got the Milwaukee blues.

Got the Milwaukee blues, got the Milwaukee blues,
I want to go west; I got the Milwaukee blues.

4. Old Bill Jones said before he died
Fix the road so the 'boes could ride
When they ride they will ride the rods
Put all their trust in the hands of God

In the hands of God, in the hands of God
They'll put all their trust in hands of God

5. Old Bill Jones said before he died,
There's two more roads he'd like to ride.
Fireman said what can it be
The Southern Pacific and the Santa Fe.

Santa Fe, yes, the Santa Fe;
The Southern Pacific and the Santa Fe.

CINDY

Cindy is a spunky little gal who has been sung about, danced to and played on all manner of stringed instruments. She first made her appearance in the early nineteenth century, probably about the time Thomas Jefferson was dusting off his wig for a stint in the White House. We can't be too sure of the exact date because she refused to reveal her age.

Frisky   **Traditional**

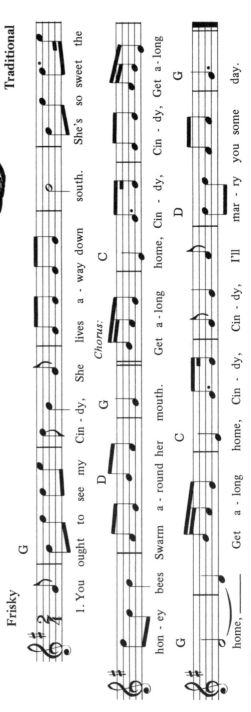

1. You ought to see my Cin - dy, She lives a - way down south. She's so sweet the hon - ey bees Swarm a - round her mouth.

Chorus: Get a - long home, Cin - dy, Get a - long home, Cin - dy, Cin - dy, Get a - long home, Cin - dy, Cin - dy, Cin - dy, I'll mar - ry you some day.

2. I wish I was an apple,
Hanging on a tree.
Every time that Cindy passed
She'd take a bite of me.

Chorus:

3. I took my Cindy to preaching
And what do you reckon she done?
She stood right up in the preacher's face
And chewed her chewing gum.

Chorus:

4. Cindy went to preaching;
She shouted all around.
She got so full of glory,
She rolled her stockings down.

Chorus:

KEEP MY SKILLET GOOD AND GREASY

Keep My Skillet Good and Greasy dates from the middle nineteenth century and has the distinction of being the first tune recorded by Uncle Dave Macon on July 8, 1924. Sing this song sassy.

Lively

Traditional

1. Gon-na buy me a sack of flour; Bake me hoe-cake ev-'ry hour,— Keep my skil-let good and greas-y all the time, time, time,...Keep my skil-let good and greas-y all the time.

2. Honey, if you say so
I'll never work no more.
I'll lay around your shanty all the time, time, time,
I'll lay around your shanty all the time.

3. Got some chickens in the sack,
Got the bloodhounds on my track.
Keep my skillet good and greasy all the time, time, time,
Keep my skillet good and greasy all the time.

4. If they beat me to the door,
I'll put 'em under the floor.
Keep my skillet good and greasy all the time, time, time,
Keep my skillet good and greasy all the time.

5. Gonna buy me a jug of brandy.
Gonna give it all to Mandy.
Keep her good and drunk and goozy all the time, time, time,
Keep her good and drunk and goozy all the time.

LITTLE STREAM OF WHISKEY

Little Stream of Whiskey, also known as *The Dying Hobo*, is a parody of the nineteenth century *Bingen on the Rhine* by Carolina E.S. Norton. It was recorded on November 6, 1926 by Burnett and Rutherford but this version was collected in Maine around 1910. The song tells of a dying hobo with a ticket to "Hobo Heaven." The line forms at the rear.

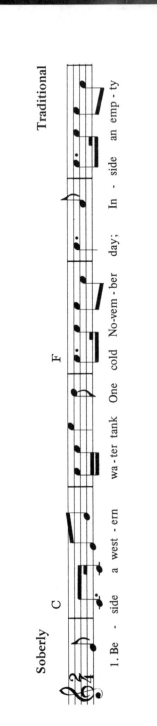

Photo by Mark V. Sanderford

Traditional

Soberly

C   F

1. Be - side   a west - ern   wa - ter tank   One cold No-vem - ber day;   In - side   an emp - ty

C   D   G   C

... box - car ... a dy - ing ... ho - bo ... lay.   His ... part - ner stood be - side him   With

F   C   G   C

low and droop-ing head, And lis-tened to the last words The dy-ing ho-bo said.

2. I'm going to a better land Where everything is bright,
Where the handouts grow on bushes And you sleep out every night.
Where you do not have to work at all Nor even change your socks;
And little streams of whiskey Come trickling down the rocks.

3. Tell my sweetheart back in Denver, That her fair face I never more will view.
Tell her that I've jumped the fast freight; And that I am going through.
Tell her not to weep for me In her eyes no tears must lurk;
For I'm gone to a better land Where I won't have to work.

4. Hark! I hear a whistle; I must catch her on the fly.
Farewell partner, it's not So hard to die.
The hobo stopped, his head fell back, He had sung his last refrain;
His partner swiped his hat and shoes And jumped the east-bound train.

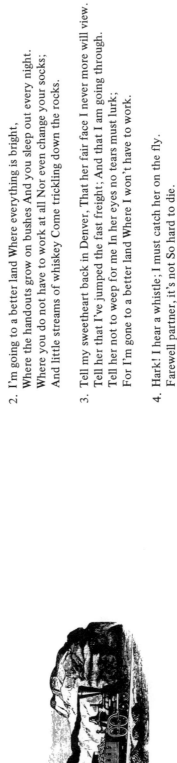

THE BALD-HEADED END OF A BROOM

Low gear

Traditional

People have been chuckling over this song for well over a hundred years. Versions have even been collected in England where the song may have originated. A nice illustration of the way that different versions come about is reflected in the first verse. Charlie Poole, who recorded the song as *Look Before You Leap* in 1930, sings the third phrase as "Like a plate of boarding house hash . . .". The English version is an interesting contrast: "Like a plate of burning hot ash . . .". If you mumble the English version, it sounds almost like Poole's rendition.

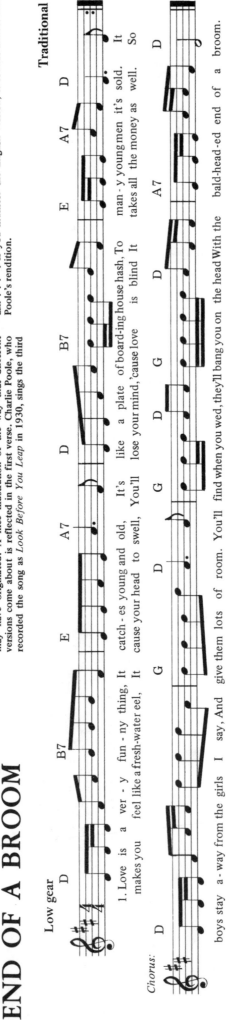

1. Love is a ver - y fun - ny thing, It catch - es young and old, It's like a plate of board-ing house hash, To man - y young men it's sold. It makes you feel like a fresh-water eel, It cause your head to swell, You'll lose your mind, 'cause love is blind It takes all the money as well. So

Chorus:

boys stay a - way from the girls I say, And give them lots of room. You'll find when you wed, they'll bang you on the head With the bald-head-ed end of a broom.

2. When you're stuck on a pretty little gal,
You talk as gentle as a dove.
You spend your money and call her honey,
To show her you're solid on love.

When your money's all gone and the rent is due,
You'll find the old saying is true.
A mole on the arm is worth two on the leg,
But what are you going to do?   *Chorus:*

3. Now, young men take my advice,
Don't be in a hurry to wed.
You'll think you're in clover 'til the honeymoon's over
And then you'll think you're dead.

With a cross-eyed baby on each knee
And a wife with a plaster on her nose.
You'll find that love don't run so smooth
When you wear your second-hand clothes. *Chorus:*

I'M THE MAN THAT RODE THE MULE AROUND THE WORLD

I'm the Man That Rode The Mule Around The World is a song either about the most unusual man who ever lived, or maybe just the biggest liar. A variant of *I Was Born 10,000 Years Ago* it probably comes from the minstrel era. This is the version recorded by Charlie Poole in his first session for Columbia records on July 27, 1925.

Sprightly

Traditional

1. I was born 4,000 years ago
   And there's nothing in this world that I don't know,
   I saw Moses on the water fighting Pharaoh and his army.
   And I can whop the man who says it isn't so. *Chorus:*

2. I saw Satan when he searched the garden o'er.
   I saw Adam and Eve driven from the door.
   The apple they were eating from the bushes I was peeping,
   I can prove it 'cause I'm the man that ate the core. *Chorus:*

3. I'm a highly educated man
   And there's things in my brain that I have planned.
   Now I been on earth so long 'til I liked to sing a song
   That old Abraham and Jacob used to say. *Chorus:*

Chorus: I'm the man who rode the mule a-round the world. ___ I'm the man who rode the mule a-round the world. ___ I rode in No-ah's ark and I'm hap-py as a lark, I'm the man who rode the mule a-round the world. ___

PAP'S BILLY GOAT

Pap's Billy Goat was learned from Currence Hammonds, an eighty year old ballad singer and teller of tall tales from Huttonsville, West Virginia. Sitting next to his wood stove, Currence sang this unaccompanied version of Pap's Billy Goat which he had learned as a boy. The last verse is the subject of a modern country song entitled I'm My Own Grandpa.

Traditional

Moderately

1. Pap-py bought him a great big bil-ly goat Ma-ma washed most ev-'ry day.
Hung their clothes out on the line. Well, the danged old goat he came that way.

2. He pulled down that old red shirt,
   You ought to hear them buttons crack.
   I'll get even with the son of a gun;
   Gonna tie him across the railroad track.

3. They tied him across the railroad track
   The train was a-comin' at a thousand rate.
   He belched up that old red shirt
   And then flagged down that danged old freight.

4. I went to the depot, bought me a ticket
   Well, I walked right in and I sit right down.
   Stuck that ticket in the brim of my hat
   Well, the doggone wind blowed it out on the ground.

5. The conductor come around and said, "Give me your ticket,"
   Well, I had to pay again or get left on the track.
   I'll get even with the son of a gun
   I've got a round trip ticket but I'm not a-comin' back.

6. The old fool, the dang fool, married me a widder.
   Well, the widder had a daughter and her name was Moll.
   Father being a widder and he married her daughter
   And now my daddy is my own son-in-law.

OLD MAID'S LAST HOPE

The Old Maid's Last Hope, commonly known as *The Burglar Man*, was written in 1887 by E.S. Thilp. This version is from the singing of West Virginia coal miner Nimrod Workman.

E. S. THILP

With feeling

1. I'll tell you a sto-ry of a bur-ga-ler man That went to rob a house. Went in the win-dow, crawled un-der the bed, Just a qui-et-ly as a mouse.—

2. About nine o'clock an old maid came in,
"I am so tired," she said.
She sat down to strip herself
And forgot to peep under the bed.

3. She took out her teeth and the big glass eye,
And the hair right off of her head.
That burglar man had nineteen fits
And he rolled out from under her bed.

4. Then from her bosom a revolver she drew
And to this burglar man said:
"You'll marry me, you burglar man,
Or I'll blow off the top of your head."

5. He looked at the teeth and the big glass eye
And he had no place to scoot.
He looked back at the bald-headed miss
And said, "Hunt for a place to shoot."

Photo by Douglas Yarrow

NIMROD WORKMAN AND PHYLLIS BOYENS

LITTLE ROSEWOOD CASKET

The beautiful, simple melody and the plaintive words to *Little Rosewood Casket* make it a classic of old-time singing. Entitled *A Package of Old Love Letters*, it was composed in 1870 by Louis P. Goullaud and C.A. White.

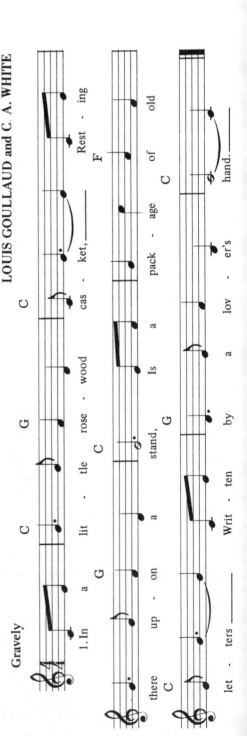

LOUIS GOULLAUD and C. A. WHITE

Gravely

1. In a lit - tle rose - wood cas - ket, Rest - ing
   up - on a stand, Is a pack - age of old
   let - ters Writ - ten by a lov - er's hand.

2. You may go and bring them, sister
   Sit down here upon my bed
   And take gently to your bosom
   My poor aching, throbbing head.

3. You have brought them, thank you sister.
   You may read them o'er to me.
   I have often tried to read them
   But for tears I could not see.

4. When I'm resting in my coffin
   And my shroud around me's wound
   And my narrow bed is ready
   In the pleasant churchyard ground.

5. Take this package of old love letters
   Strew them all around my heart.
   But this little ring he gave me
   From my finger never part.

6. I must say farewell, dear sister,
   Place my hands upon my breast.
   I am dying, kiss me sister,
   I am going home to rest.

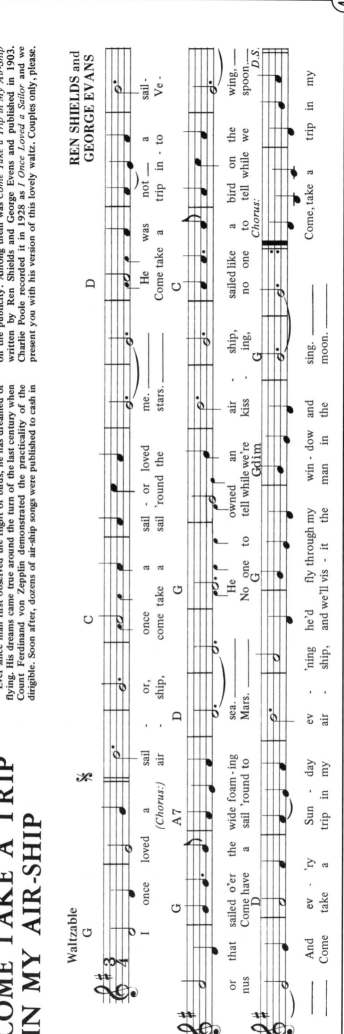

COME TAKE A TRIP IN MY AIR-SHIP

Ever since man first observed the flight of birds, he has dreamed of flying. His dreams came true around the turn of the last century when Count Ferdinand von Zepplin demonstrated the practicality of the dirigible. Soon after, dozens of air-ship songs were published to cash in on the publicity. Among them was *Come Take a Trip in My Air-Ship* written by Ren Shields and George Evens and published in 1903. Charlie Poole recorded it in 1928 as *I Once Loved a Sailor* and we present you with his version of this lovely waltz. Couples only, please.

REN SHIELDS and GEORGE EVANS

HARD TIMES COME AGAIN NO MORE

STEPHEN C. FOSTER

Hard Times Come Again No More was written by Stephen Foster and published in 1855. Apparently, it was based partly on fragments he heard from the family housekeeper, Olivia Pise, who learned it in the black church where she worshipped. Although it was not one of Foster's more successful compositions, it was, in fact, one of his favorites. In his last days he could often be found singing *Hard Times Come Again No More.*

Moderato

Let us pause in life's plea-sures and count its man-y tears While we all sup sor-row with the poor: There's a song that will lin-ger for-ev-er in our ears; Oh! Hard times, come a-gain no more.

Chorus:

Hard times, hard times, come a-gain no more; Man-y days you have lin-gered a-round my cab-in door, Oh! Hard times, come a-gain no more.

It's the song, the sigh of the wea-ry;

2. While we seek mirth and beauty and music light and gay
There are frail forms fainting at the door:
Though their voices are silent, their pleading looks will say,
Oh! Hard times, come again no more.   *Chorus.*

3. There's a pale drooping maiden who toils her life away
With a worn heart whose better days are o'er.
Though her voice would be merry, it's sighing all the day,
Oh! Hard times, come again no more.   *Chorus:*

4. It's a sigh that is wafted across the troubled wave;
It's a wail that is heard upon the shore;
It's a dirge that is murmured around the lowly grave;
Oh! Hard times, come again no more.   *Chorus:*

WILD BILL JONES

The first recording of *Wild Bill Jones* was made by Samantha Bumgarner and Eva Davis for Columbia in April of 1924. Although no scholar has ever tracked down the whereabouts of the real Wild Bill Jones, his legend remains intact. The last verse can be sung as a chorus.

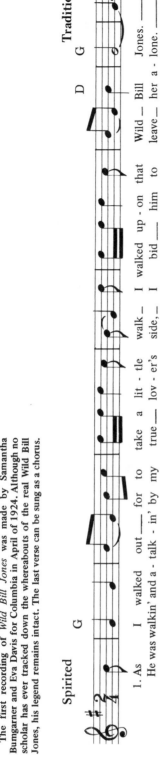

Spirited

Traditional

1. As I walked out ___ for to take a lit - tle walk ___ I walked up - on that Wild ___ Bill Jones. ___
He was walkin' and a - talk - in' by my true ___ lov - er's side, ___ I bid ___ him to leave ___ her a - lone. ___

2. He said his age, it is 21.
Too old for to be controlled.
I pulled my revolver from my side
And I destroyed that poor boy's soul.

3. He reeled and he staggered and he fell to the ground
And he gave one dying groan
I threw my arms around my darlin's neck
Saying, baby, won't you please come home.

4. They sent me to prison for twenty long years,
This poor boy longs to be free
But Wild Bill Jones and that long neck bottle
Has made a ruin of me.

5. So pass around that long neck bottle,
And we'll all go on a spree.
For today was the last of that Wild Bill Jones
And tomorrow is the last of me.

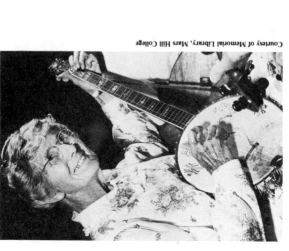

SAMANTHA BUMGARNER

CLUCK OLD HEN

Songs about chickens have always been popular in old-time music. Perhaps this is because with a little prodding a fiddle can be made to sound like the squawking of a chicken. *Cluck Old Hen* is made up of interchangeable verses. The first verse is currently sung around North Carolina. The verse about the "taters" is with the compliments of Frank Profitt and the last verse comes from Tommy Jarrell.

Courtesy of The Library of Congress

Traditional

Sprightly

My old hen's a good old hen, She lays eggs for the rail - road men.
Some - times eight, some - times ten, That's e - nough for the rail - road men.

Chorus:

Cluck old hen, cluck and sing. Ain't laid an egg since way — last spring.
Cluck old hen, cluck and squall. Ain't laid an egg since way — last fall.

2. First time she cackled, she cackled in the pot
Next time she cackled, she cackled in the lot.
My old hen, she won't do
She lays eggs and taters too.   *Chorus:*

3. Had a little hen, she had a wooden leg
The best dang hen that ever laid an egg.
Lay more eggs than any hen around the barn
Another little drink wouldn't do me any harm.   *Chorus:*

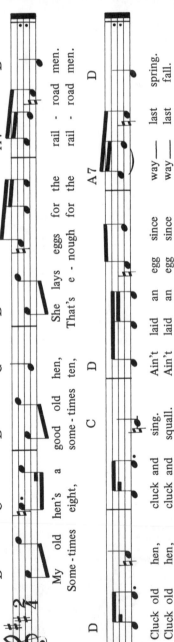

MOLE IN THE GROUND

Whoever composed this song must have been feeling mighty lonesome to want to be a mole in the ground. It was first recorded by Bascomb Lamar Lunsford on March 15, 1924 and was one of the first examples of old-time banjo music to be put on record. Lunsford learned it from Fred Moody of Haywood County, North Carolina, in 1901. The word "bend" in the third verse is often incorrectly sung "pen." "Bend" apparently refers to the bend in the Pigeon river well known as a haven for "the rough and rowdy men."

Lonesome

Traditional

1. I wish I was a mole in the ground. I wish I was a mole in the ground. If I's a mole in the ground I'd root this moun-tain down, I wish I was a mole in the ground.

2. Kempie wants a nine-dollar shawl,
Yes, Kempie wants a nine-dollar shawl.
When I come over the hill with a forty-dollar bill,
And it's honey, where you been so long?

3. Where have you been so long?
Yes, where have you been so long?
I've been in the bend with the rough and rowdy men,
And it's honey, where you been so long?

4. Oh, I don't like a railroad man..
No, I don't like a railroad man.
A railroad man will kill you when he can
And he'll drink up your blood like wine.

5. I wish I was a lizard in the spring.
Yes, I wish I was a lizard in the spring.
If I was a lizard in the spring I could hear my darling sing,
And I wish I was a lizard in the spring.

Photo by Wayne Erbsen

WALTER DAVIS

SUGAR BABE

Sugar Babe has a beautiful, haunting melody that takes you deep into the mountains of West Virginia, where this version comes from. A variant of *Red Apple Juice* and *Red Rocking Chair*, it sounds best with sparse instrumentation.

Traditional

Woefully

Some old round - er come a - long, Took my sug - ar babe — and gone. And I ain't got no

sug - ar ba - by now. _____ No, I ain't got no sug - ar ba - by now. _____

2. I gave her every cent I made,
And I laid her in the shade.
And I ain't got no sugar baby now.
No, I ain't got no sugar baby now.

3. It's who'll call you honey
And it's who'll sing this song?
And it's who'll rock the cradle when I'm gone?
Who'll rock the cradle when I'm gone?

4. I ain't got no use for
Your red rocking chair.
And I ain't got no sugar baby now.
No, I ain't got no sugar baby now.

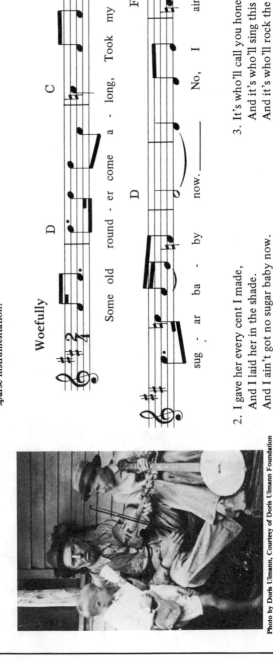

Photo by Doris Ulmann, Courtesy of Doris Ulmann Foundation

SHADY GROVE

Shady Grove is a favorite song of the mountains. Also called *Little Betty Ann*, it is composed mainly of verses which "float" from one song to another.

Traditional

Photo by Doris Ulmann, Courtesy of Doris Ulmann Foundation

Loping

Chorus: Dm

Dm   C

Shad - y Grove, my li'l love,

Shad - y Grove, I say.

F   C   Dm   A7   Dm

Shad - y Grove, my li'l love,

I'm a - goin' a - way.

1. I went to see my Shady Grove
Standing in the door;
Shoes and stockings in her hands,
Little bare feet on the floor.
Chorus:

2. Peaches in the summertime;
Apples in the fall.
If I can't get the girl I love,
I won't have none at all.
Chorus:

3. Sixteen horses in my team,
The leader he is blind.
Ever I travel this road again,
There'll be trouble on my mind.
Chorus:

4. Fifteen miles of mountain road,
Twenty miles of sand;
If ever I travel this road again
I'll be a married man.
Chorus:

DON'T YOU HEAR JERUSALEM MOAN?

Don't You Hear Jerusalem Moan? is an old gospel/novelty song that manages to poke fun at several of the major religions. As if the words weren't enough to make this song outrageous, the chorus has a few extra beats added for good measure. This version comes to us from the inimitable Skillet Lickers.

GID TANNER AND HIS SKILLET-LICKERS

Traditional

Snappy

1. Well, the Meth-od-ist preach-er, you can tell him where he go; Don't you hear Je-ru-sa-lem moan? Don't –

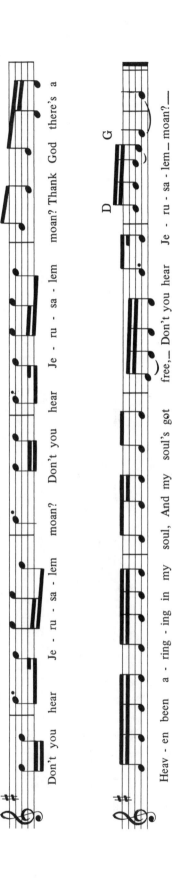

Chorus:

G | G | C | G

Don't you hear Je - ru - sa - lem moan? Don't you hear Je - ru - sa - lem moan? Thank God there's a

D | G

Heav - en been a - ring - ing in my soul, And my soul's got free,— Don't you hear Je - ru - sa - lem— moan?—

2. Well, the Baptist preacher you can tell him by his coat;
   Don't you hear Jerusalem moan?
   Has a bottle in his pocket and he can hardly tote
   Don't you hear Jerusalem moan?

   Chorus:

3. Well, the Holy Roller preacher sure am a sight
   Don't you hear Jerusalem moan?
   Well, he gets 'em all a-rolling and he kicks out the light
   Don't you hear Jerusalem moan?

   Chorus:

4. Well, the Presbyterian preacher he lives in town;
   Don't you hear Jerusalem moan?
   Neck's so stiff he can hardly look around;
   Don't you hear Jerusalem moan?

   Chorus:

SHALL WE GATHER AT THE RIVER?

ROBERT LOWRY

Shall We Gather at the River is an old-time gospel song written by Robert Lowry in 1864. It was first recorded on May 10, 1927 by the Dixie Sacred Singers composed of Uncle Dave Macon, along with Sam and Kirk McGee. It was, incidently, one of Uncle Dave's favorite hymns.

2. On the margin of the river,
   Washing up its silver spray,
   We will walk and worship ever,
   All the happy golden day.

   Chorus:

3. There we reach the shining river,
   Lay we every burden down.
   Grace our spirits will deliver,
   And provide a robe and crown.

   Chorus:

4. Soon we'll reach the shining river,
   Soon our pilgrimage will cease,
   Soon our happy hearts will quiver,
   With the melody of peace.

   Chorus: